50 Tips for Breaking into the Modeling Industry

By

Jennifer McLeod

ISBN: 1-4033-4132-X (e-book)
ISBN: 1-4033-4133-8 (Paperback)

This book is printed on acid free paper.

1stBooks - rev. 6/3/03

ACKNOWLEDGEMENTS

Praise is extended to God for giving me the ability and foresight of creation. Honor is extended to my family for always supporting and believing in me. It takes a village to raise a child, so thank you to all personal friends and associates who have helped me grow along the way. May peace be with you and your blessings be manifold.

INTRODUCTION

When I was a little girl I used to dream of having a closet full of beautiful dresses. I even wanted my parents to buy a magic wand for me so I could wave the wand and fill my closest with gowns. I began modeling and competed in my first pageant at the age of two. As a teenager I participated in extracurricular sports and activities, attended modeling schools, studied the fashion industry and continued competing in pageants.

Throughout the years I have traveled many paths and encountered many surprises, in the modeling industry, which have all been learning experiences. This book serves as a quick reference, pocket guide to help you get started as a model.

My hope is that you'll take at least one helpful idea from this book in a fraction of the time I spent learning it. Best of Luck!

TABLE OF CONTENTS

1.

Tips for Recognizing Today's Model

1. **DETERMINE WHICH CATEGORY OF MODELING IS RIGHT FOR YOU.**

The modeling industry is broken into various categories that range in requirement, pay and competition.

The largest amount of money goes to the world's **Supermodels**. A super model is a model whose name is a household name. Supermodels generally stand at least 5'9 and have beautiful bodies and perfect facial features. These models can make a generous living from modeling alone. Approximately 5% of models who attempt to model will achieve supermodel status.

"Talkers are no good doers." William Shakespeare

High Fashion Models have the highest visibility in the industry. These models grace fashion magazine covers, fashion billboards and fashion television commercials on a regular basis. Female models in this category are generally required to be 14-19 years of age, with a minimum height of 5'9. Attractive looks and body proportion are essential. The pay is high and not uncommon for a single campaign to pay a million dollars plus.

Runway Models must be at least 5'9 and have slender bodies proportionate to their height. Ages can range from 14-on. Rates of pay are negotiated according to the professional status of the model and typically range from $500-$5000 per show. Runway shows occur twice a year (typically during Fall and Spring) and fashions circulate from Milan to London, to Paris, to New York, and then to other American markets.

"The final forming of a person's character lies in their own hands." *Anne Frank*

Print (Catalog, Fashion Advertising, Editorial)

Models range from the highest paid supermodels gracing the pages of international major catalogs to those seen in newspaper inserts for local major retailers. Most retail ads are shot in the city where the corporate headquarters are located. Requirements for print and catalog models include great skin, great smile and an attractive and proportionate body. Females are typically 5'8-5'11 and wear a size 6-8, with ages ranging from 15-on. Major catalogs can pay $10,000 to $15,000 per day for top models compared to local department retailers who pay roughly between $100-$200 per hour.

"Thoughts are energy, and you can make your world or break your world by your thinking." *Susan L. Taylor*

Commercial Print Models can be different shapes and sizes depending on the specific look the advertisers are seeking. This category is also known as product print category. The pay for commercial print modeling, however, may not be enough to make a living.

"In the long run men hit only what they aim at." *Henry David Thoreau*

Informal Models are usually hired to promote a product, a store opening or a new line of clothing. Models in this category typically work in boutiques, shopping malls, retail stores or even in private homes. Informal Models are expected to show the clothing well and speak intelligently about the product they are promoting. They must be able to attract potential customers as well as answer any questions that the customers may have. Informal models either freelance or work with a specific company. The pay varies according to the job and rivals print modeling rates.

"Great works are performed not by strength but by perseverance." *Samuel Jackson*

Promotional (Swimsuit, Beauty or Spokesperson) Models are live models. Live models perform and interact with a live audience. They typically have very attractive features and outgoing personalities. Hip requirements are not strict, although a promotional model's body must be proportionate and in excellent shape. Height requirements are generally at least 5'. Sporting Event, Car Show and In-Store Promotional models are good examples of this category. The pay varies widely.

"No one will do it for you." Ben Stein

Illustration Models must have attractive features with an attractive body proportionate in height and weight. Illustration models pose for extended periods of time for designers or advertisers who are sketching. They also may pose for painters or sculptors who are working on an art piece for a gallery. Before photographs became popular, illustration was a common form of advertising. Illustration also allows an illustrator to slightly change the pose of the model. Rates of pay vary.

"Make no little plans; they have no magic to stir men's blood…make big plans, aim high in hope and work."
Daniel H. Burnham

Trade and Convention Show Models must have an outgoing, positive, well-rounded personality, excellent sales and communication skills, and attractive looks. Age and height requirements vary. Convention models typically serve as hosts, who help promote an individual company or product by passing out literature, determining potential customers and speaking with the public. Trade and Convention Show models may also be employed as demonstrators or narrators, in which case they may be required, to use an ear prompter or memorize a script. Demonstrators and narrators are paid the highest rates among Trade and Convention Show Models. This pay rate is typically higher than that for Editorial and Promotional models.

"The way to do things is to begin." *Horace Greely*

Petite Models are generally between the height of 5'3 and 5'6 and weigh between 100 and 110 pounds. Most petite models will work in print and television commercials.

Plus Size Models vary in size, but 13 is the average size. Plus size models are generally older than 30 years of age, but agencies welcome younger models that are between the ages of 19-30. Height requirements range between 5'8-5'10.

"A model is the ultimate salesperson to the masses."
Eileen Ford

2. STUDY TODAY'S MODELING MARKET TRENDS.

Once you have determined where you fit into the modeling industry, study the modeling markets to find role models and visualize where you see yourself working. Study magazines, television, billboards, and the Internet to learn what is current in the modeling industry. Seek the top level of professionalism in the industry to develop a feel for top-level professional work. These studies will help you stay current and evolve.

3. STUDY THE COMPETITION.

After you've determined the type of model you are and where you see yourself working, look through different media channels (magazines, film, television, the Internet, fashion trade shows etc.) and find your competition. How do you measure up to your competition in the industry? What can you do to improve your level of professionalism as a model?

"Spiritual force is stronger than material force; thoughts rule the world." *Ralph Waldo Emerson*

4.   VALUE YOUR TIME AND RESOURCES.

Know your own self-worth. Thoroughly research any agency with which you choose to associate. One way to determine the legitimacy of agencies is to contact the Screen Actors Guild office and find out if the agent is franchised. Only legitimate agencies are franchised and to maintain franchise status the agency must adhere to a set of professional industry standards in business dealings. You may also want to contact the Better Business Bureau to ask questions regarding a particular agency or modeling organization. The contact information for the Screen Actors Guild is located in Section Five of this publication.

5.   STAY TRUE TO YOURSELF.

Learn who you are as a person and project that personality into your modeling career.

"If you want to be respected you must respect yourself."
Spanish Proverb

6.   BE RESPONSIBLE.

One influential, world champion Taekwon-Do Master defines responsibility as "Doing what you are supposed to do, when you are supposed to do it, whether you like it or not" Be dependable and reliable. When an agent calls you for work you must be available to go on castings and to accept modeling jobs. Remember, you are representing the reputable name of your agency as well as yourself.

7.   DEVELOP SELF-DISCIPLINE.

A model is paid and expected to be healthy. It is your job to have a fit figure, to have beautiful skin, a radiant smile and a sparkling personality. Each category of modeling requires different physical characteristics. Learn those characteristics and discipline yourself to maintain those characteristics. Develop the discipline to have balanced health. Get plenty of rest the night before a big job, so that you will be at your best.

"Death is certain and life too short to live in the mediocrity of trying." *Anonymous*

8.   RADIATE A POSITIVE ATTITUDE AND SELF CONFIDENCE.

The modeling industry is full of people who like to work with other people who are positive, professional, can deliver, are on time and do not complain. Production crews, advertising agencies, photographers and booking agents are all under pressure to complete projects in a timely manner, for what can be a tremendous amount of money. Complaining or having a negative attitude will add to the stress of other people's jobs and create an undesirable reputation around your name. Help the job to go more smoothly by being prepared, in knowing appropriate camera angles, lighting directions, stage directions, marks and cues. Know what is expected from you to make other people's job easier. This will create a positive buzz around your name, increasing the likelihood of requests to work with you again, and referrals to other people about working with you.

"Happiness is a habit…cultivate it." Elbert Hubbard

9.   ENJOY THE PROCESS.

A career in the modeling industry is a process. Few are fortunate enough to achieve overnight success and most successful careers are the result of commitment, discipline, desire, faith and hard work. If you truly want to be a model, commit to the process and enjoy the process along the way. Know that with each step you are growing and have learned more than you knew yesterday. One talent manager stated that to achieve "star" or top billing status takes an average of ten years.

"Problems are only opportunities in work clothes."
Frederick R. Koppel

11.

Tips for Committing to Mental Health

10.   DEVELOP HIGH SELF ESTEEM.

As a model, you must be your own source of authority and confidence. The camera will recognize your emotions as well as how you feel about yourself. You must be able to project attitude both to the camera and to a live audience.

11.   ACCEPT REJECTION.

Just because you do not get a job after you have auditioned, do not take it personally. You may simply be too tall, too short, have a different body type, a different ethnicity, different hair color, different eye color or different personality than that for which they are looking. Remember, the more "no's" you get the closer you are to a" yes". Learn from your rejections and evaluate how you can improve your skills. Take that improvement with you to the next audition.

"Talk is cheap; lip service free; we shall see what is to be." *Anonymous*

12. SET REALISTIC GOALS.

Overnight success is possible, however, perseverance and unshakable commitment are more realistic in aiding you to attain your goals as a model. Write your goals down with a realistic, balanced timeline in mind. Review your goals daily and revise your goals as you go through life's changes. The following is an example of a structure for goal setting. Remember to begin with the end in mind:

Write five goals pertaining to personal and family relationships that you hope to achieve in the next one-five years. These will serve as a motivation for why you do what you do.

What are the short-term steps you need to take in the next three months, six months, nine months and twelve months to achieve these goals?

Write five goals pertaining to self-improvement that you hope to achieve in the next one-five years. These will serve as a motivation for what you need to do.

What are the short-term steps you need to take in the next three months, six months, nine months and twelve months to achieve these goals?

Write five goals pertaining to your career and your professional life you hope to achieve in the next one-ten years. These goals will serve as the motivation as to how you manifest what you do and why you do what you do.

What are the short-term steps you need to take in the next three months, six months, nine months and twelve months to achieve these goals?

Review your goals every three-six months to see if you are on track and which goals may need revising due to life-altering situations.

13.   JOURNAL FOR SANITY.

Keeping a journal of your journey as a model will serve as a great source of inspiration. Writing down stories of your events during each day will help you maintain your motivation. When you are feeling discouraged, go to your journal and read about what you have accomplished. Expository or free-flowing writing will give you insight to who you are as a person, furthermore, and it will help you develop your own true image. Begin a personal portfolio of your work for your own use, in addition to your professional portfolio. The following sheet is an example of a journal page with observations that you may want to record on a daily basis:

JOURNALING FOR BALANCE, CLARITY AND AWARENESS

Date:

Water (at least ½ gallon):

Vitamins/Medication:

Exercise/Weight:

Mood/Emotion (on a scale of one to ten):

Daily Events:

Wardrobe:

People I met and how I met them:

Names of people I helped today and how:

Compliments I received today:

What I did to advance my career today:

Definition of a new word I learned today:

The five blessings I am most thankful for today:

14.   BUILD A SUPPORT TEAM.

Form a team of supportive people who encourage your vision of being a model. Seek mentors who live a life you respect and admire. Learn as much as you can from these people. Do not waste your precious time with negative people. They will only infect your attitude. People who support your vision will give you an uplifted feeling and be delighted in your successes.

15.   SURROUND YOURSELF WITH POSITIVE AND LIKE-MINDED PEOPLE.

One manager of an international star said, "Artists *like* other Artists" As a model you are an artist and part of the arts community. You will work with amazing photographers, painters, sculptors, designers, producers, and directors. Select positive and like-minded peers in the modeling industry, as well as the arts and entertainment community.

"Energy is the power that drives every human being. It is not lost by exertion but maintained by it." *Germaine Greer*

16.   EDUCATE YOURSELF.

Knowledge of your industry will help you to stay motivated. Top models in demand are models who are professional, have an outgoing personality and are fun on the set. The more you know about your industry, the more you will have to talk about on the set, and the more you will develop an appreciation for the fellow crew members with whom you are working. Exercise your brain. You will be knowledgeable in a wide range of subjects and able to carry on a conversation with nearly anyone. You must learn the appropriate questions to ask if someone is speaking to you on a subject with which you are unfamiliar. Learn to speak proper English, technical English and Spanish. For further expansion, consider learning other languages. Be aware of varying degrees of dialects. Be able to relate to a wide array of people.

"A life being very short, and the quiet hours of it few, we ought to waste none of them reading valueless books."
John Ruskin

17.   CULTIVATE THE ART OF LISTENING.

Several industry behind-the-scenes people have mentioned frustration with models and talent who do not take direction well. Learn to listen to what you are being asked to do, then do it.

18.   KEEP AN OPEN MIND.

As a professional model you will travel and interact with people from diverse cultures and lifestyles. By keeping an open mind on all subjects, you allow room for learning from others. Diversity will broaden your perception of the world.

"Beauty is in the eye of the beholder." *Margaret Wolfe Hungerford*

19. LIVE IN THE MOMENT.

Sometimes the future or the present can consume you. The true moment is now. Remember that each day may be your last day and seek to be fulfilled in that day as if it was your last. Be a model everyday. Great joy comes from living in the moment. Be here now.

20. BE GRACIOUS.

People will help you along the way. Appreciate those people and events. Do not take your position or talent for granted. Remember that others' belief in you and kindness have helped you get where you are. They are precious; treat them as such. One way to combat arrogance is through education and humility. Arrogance is defined as ego + ignorance.

"Accept the challenges so that you may feel the exhilaration of victory." *General George S. Patton*

21.   BE KIND AND COMPASSIONATE.

If you are kind to others they usually will meet you with the same kindness. No one wants to work with an unpleasant or inconsiderate person. Think of situations from the other person's point of view. Be aware of how you are coming across in conversation. Learn to empathize.

"Hitch your wagon to a star." *Ralph Waldo Emmerson*

22. DEVELOP SOUND ACCOUNTING HABITS.

These habits will serve you well as you become more established and begin dealing with larger pay rates for your work. Begin to keep your receipts and track your expenses. Many are tax deductible. As a model you will probably be self-employed as an independent contractor. You also may want to consider having a flexible part-time job for slower periods in your career.

You will need to develop a financial cushion, since modeling work is sporadic. However, remember you must make yourself available for auditions and bookings. Some suggestions for flexible part-time work include substitute teaching, restaurant service, and sales positions. Be sure to discuss with any part-time employer your situation as a model. Some employers are willing to work with you; some are not. If they are not willing to work with you then they are not the right employer for you. Establishing a financial cushion also enables you to make quality career choices, as opposed to taking whatever comes your way because you need the money. The following is a list of tax deductible items for which you may qualify. Discuss your financial situation with a trusted professional tax attorney or financial specialist.

Your personal tax consultant or financial specialist will best know updates and current allowances. As a model, you are responsible for overall record-keeping and documentation. Keep track of income by opening a separate checking account to deposit the income received as an independent contractor through performing. At the end of the year, a 1099 should be received if income has totaled over $600 for that calendar year. Keep deduction envelopes marked to avoid having to go through receipts at the end of the year. Income tax is payable on net income or all the money left after expenses have been deducted.

Deductible Expenses:

- **Accounting fees**
- **Agency fees or commissions**
- **Cosmetics**
- **Dues and publications**
- **Educational seminars, training, coaching, exercise facilities**
- **Entertainment** (50% of the cost of entertaining)

  Substantiated by recording:

  a) Who-the person you entertained, the business relationship to you

  b) When-the date the entertainment took place

  c) Where-the place you went when entertaining

  d) Why-The reason for entertaining and the benefit expected

- **Equipment** (fax machine, computer, etc.)
- **Postage and courier expenses**
- **Gifts** (less than $25 per person)
- **Grooming** (hair, nails, spa, facials, etc.)
- **Miscellaneous office expenses and supplies**

- **Auto expenses** ($.34 per mile-keep an auto log in the glove box of your car)

- **Prints, composites, portfolio costs**

- **Taxis and public transportation**

- **Travel** (must be one year or less in duration and you must maintain your original residency). Air fares and local transportation, hotels and lodging, car rental, meals (only if the trip requires overnight stay)

- **Wardrobe** (Dry-cleaning of clothes for a specific booking or clothing not suitable for every day wear)

23.   ATTAIN BALANCE THROUGH SPIRITUALITY.

Consider yoga, martial arts, spending time in nature and/or praying. The modeling industry is a very fast-paced industry with large degrees of uncertainty. Finding an activity that creates balance of self will be of great benefit to you. Since the industry is chaotic, you must be stable and centered. Yoga and martial arts are excellent choices because they exercise a combination of mental, physical and spiritual energies. Seek activities that involve your entire being.

"You have got to make it happen." *Joe Greene*

III.

Tips for Committing to Physical Health

Jennifer McLeod

24. PRACTICE GOOD NUTRITION.

You may want to consider speaking with a professional nutritionist. If you prefer, you can do the research on your own by keeping a log of your weight, measurements and the way your body reacts to different foods. This will help you to determine if you have any food allergies or which foods may cause your skin to break out or may cause you to gain weight. Next, research the library and Internet regarding nutrition and determine an optimum eating lifestyle. After you have determined this eating lifestyle, talk it over with a nutrition professional to make sure your plan is sound for balanced health.

"Life gives nothing to a man without labor." *Horace*

25. EXERCISE.

You may want to hire a personal trainer if you are unsure about an optimum exercise routine. Exercise will keep your body physically fit, as well as improve oxygen to the brain, which will improve your attitude and thought process. Running and walking are among the top exercises for overall body work out. If you are disciplined enough, however, a blend of aerobic exercise and weight-lifting, three to five days per week for one hour may help you stay in optimum physical health. Resistance training is also excellent for maintaining body tone. Consult with your physician or personal trainer to learn a routine best suited to you and your individual needs. Find exercise activities that you enjoy and are fun. Stretching is important to keeping your body free of tension and relaxed. Being relaxed in front of the camera is critical to your success as a model. Stretching also protects your muscles from injury while exercising. Stretch before and after exercising.

"You must begin to think of yourself as the person you want to be." *David Viscott*

26.   CARE FOR YOUR SKIN.

Develop a skin care routine, including a thorough cleansing of your entire body morning and evening. Exfoliates can be helpful in removing dead skin cells. Using a loofa on your body will remove the top layer of skin cells revealing smoother, more radiant skin. Applying a facial mask twice a week will help your skin tone to remain even and create a glowing, youthful look. Having a facial once a month will also help your skin to glow. Consult with a skin care professional regarding such services to learn which products work best for your skin type. Apply moisturizer to both your entire body and face after bathing. Wear sunscreen when outdoors. Treat yourself to a manicure and pedicure every two weeks to keep your hands and feet attractive.

"If you don't run your own life, somebody else will."
John Atkinson

27. CARE FOR YOUR HAIR.

Determine a hairstyle, shape and color that are complimentary to the structure of your face, and allow for versatility in looks. Consider which style is suitable for your texture of hair. Determine how much maintenance and time you are willing give to your hair. Do not over-process your hair. Ask your agent for a list of reputable salons in your area and then make an appointment for a consultation. You may want to speak to other clients of the salon to determine the satisfaction level, especially if you are coloring, perming or relaxing your hair. Once you choose a stylist and a style that you like, keep your hair trimmed every six-nine weeks and, if you can afford it, deep conditioned by your stylist once a month. You may also want to consider using an intensive conditioner once a week at home. Your stylist will help you determine which products are best for your individual hair needs.

"The shortest answer is doing." *English Proverb*

28.   MAKE UP YOUR FACE.

One skin care professional claims," The best make-up is beautiful skin." Keep your face clean. When choosing a foundation, have a professional at a make-up counter test your skin tone to find a perfect match of foundation. Even the slightest deviation in tone may be noticeably unattractive. Strive to find make-up that enhances, not covers. Use your skin care routine to take care of temporary blemishes. Consult with professional beauty advisors to determine which colors are best for your skin tone. Seek make-up that allows your skin to breath. Have a professional make-over so you can learn how to most effectively apply your make-up from day to evening, from color to black-and-white photos, and from live performances to on-camera appearances. Professional lines and discounts are available specifically for fashion, art and entertainment industry professionals.

"Doubt whom you will, but never yourself." *Christine Bowee*

29. AVOID ILLEGAL DRUGS AND DRINK ALCOHOL ONLY IN RESPONSIBLE MODERATION.

Alcohol is a depressant and can speed the aging process. Your body is your product. Treat it well. Drugs change the chemistry of your brain and impede wise career choices as well as performances. Drugs will destroy your career and your life. Drink legally and responsibly. Arrange for a designated driver, taxi or car service; do not drink and drive. Keep cards of driving services in your wallet.

"Why not go out on a limb, isn't that where the fruit is?" *Frank Scully*

30.   PROTECT YOURSELF AND BE SAFE.

Verify any person who approaches you regarding work as a model. Do not go anywhere, especially to distant locations, with any person or crew claiming to be a photographer, producer, agent, public relations coordinator, etc. without first verifying their reputable existence. You can call your local agencies and industry unions as well as police stations for personal verification. Preserve full mental capacity when around strangers by not drinking so that you are always ready to make the best decision regarding your life and well being. If anything out of the ordinary occurs while you are working on an assignment or at an audition, or if anyone asks you unexpectedly to disrobe, notify your agent or the proper authorities immediately. Take a self defense course.

"Every man is the architect of his own fortune." *Appius Claudius*

IV.

Tips for Creating Your Professional Modeling Image

31. DEVELOP YOUR OWN STYLE.

Look through magazines and billboards, and at film and television to identify with images that are reflective of you. Some popular style categories include Glamorous, Classic, Vintage, Trendy, Funky and Outdoorsy. Fashion and lifestyle magazines are good places to start. You may want to combine a few styles to complete your personal style statement.

"Life is what your thoughts make it." *Marcus Aurelius*

32.   BUILD YOUR WARDROBE TO LAST.

Once you've determined the style which best reflects you, begin to build your wardrobe with pieces that will last. Generally speaking, classic displays of your personal style are the best. Avoid fad fashion. Even if your style is funky, trendy or glamorous, choose items that you may be able to wear at least two years from the original date of purchase. You must begin to build your wardrobe with basics and then build upon those basics to accentuate and emphasize your personal style. You must build a specific section of your wardrobe, which you will wear to your auditions. Occasionally, you will wear pieces of your own wardrobe while working.

"If there is no wind, row." *Latin Proverb*

33. DEMONSTRATE PROFESSIONAL ETIQUETTE AND COURTESY.

Study appropriate business behavior. Consider taking classes in etiquette. Avoid chewing gum while on castings or while interacting with clients. Do not smoke or eat while you are on an assignment. Do not discuss pay or salary with other models on the set. Discussion of pay can create an uncomfortable work environment. It is appropriate, however, to connect with other models and to begin building your network of industry professionals. After you have completed each assignment or casting, it is appropriate to send a thank-you note to the production crew or advertising agency. It is also appropriate to send thank-you notes to your agent, as without them sending you on the casting, you would not have got the job. You must, however, find the fine line between being gracious and being over-gracious.

"Light tomorrow with today!" *Elizabeth Barrett Browning*

34. NURTURE INDUSTRY RELATIONSHIPS.

Once you've begun to develop your network of industry professionals, you must develop a system to stay in the forefront of their minds. If you are staying busy in your career by taking new photos and adding to your talents with acting, singing or dance classes, it is appropriate to let the people in your network of industry professionals know. Let them know about community projects in which you are also involved. Create a mailing list and keep in contact with your network at least once every six months.

35. BE A PROFESSIONAL AT ALL TIMES.

In this industry, *who* knows *you* is as important as *what* you know. Because you are a professional model, people you have never met may recognize your face. Keep this in mind while you are out socializing and traveling. The person next to you may be your next client or a relative of your previous client. Act accordingly.

"They can do all because they think they can." *Virgil*

36. BE LIKEABLE AND PERSONABLE.

Be interested in the people with whom you are working and make notes, so that next time you work with this person you will have plenty to talk about during down moments in production. One industry professional advises to "Be interested, not interesting."

37. GET INVOLVED-PAGEANTS CAN HELP YOU GET STARTED.

Find local pageants in your community. Often agents will attend or judge these pageants in search of new talent. Call your local Chamber of Commerce or look up pageants on the Internet. You may want to phone legitimate modeling agencies in your area and ask if they have a list of local pageants that they would be willing to share with you. Verify the legitimacy of any pageant you choose.

"Be not simply good; be good for something." *Thoreau*

38.   LEARN HOW THE AGENCY AND YOUR AGENT WORKS.

Each agent and agency will operate differently. Once you sign with an agent, the agency will normally give you their code of conduct. This will include the public image the agency wants you to project, as well as professional behaviors that you are expected to uphold. Study this and act accordingly to create a harmonious relationship between your agency and/or agents.

39.   FIND AN AGENT WHO IS RIGHT FOR YOU.

Submit and interview. Different agencies specialize in different types of looks and personalities. This is why it is important to determine your personal image and style so that you can seek an agent who is also seeking you. Your rate of success will be higher if you know an agency is looking for your type at the time that you submit for an interview.

"When you bombard yourself with inward success, you don't have time to be negative." *Frank Meyer*

40. DOCUMENT AUDITIONS, CASTINGS AND "GO SEES".

Write down your thoughts regarding each agency interview, casting and job so that you can refer to your notes when working for a client again. This can also help you identify self-defeating patterns and blocks that may be standing in your way of getting work or an agent. The following pages include a sample form for documenting castings and bookings.

BOOKING/CASTING/INTERVIEW LOG

Date:

Referred by:

Type of event:

Clothing line/Product line:

Casting Director:

Name of Company or Agency:

Address and phone number:

Name of contact and title:

Company's specialty:

Directions:

Time to arrive:

Mileage:

Marketing tools given to the company:

Interviewer's comments:

Wardrobe, hair and make up I presented:

What I will do differently next time:

What I did well:

Dates of follow-up contact:

Other contacts or leads resulting from this event:

41.   TRAVEL LIGHT. LEARN ESSENTIALS.

When traveling, take only what you need for the number of days that you will be traveling. Include basic-colored, comfortable clothes that easily complement each other. Choose colors that complement your skin tone so that you will look your best. Generally, jersey and knit materials are a wise choice because they do not wrinkle easily. In general, for a one-week stay, you can get by with one pair of evening shoes and one pair of daytime shoes. Choose simple accessories, undergarments and make-up that work with all of your travel pieces. Having a complete model tote is essential to your success. The tote includes tools needed in preparation for your work. Consider investing in two pieces of hard sided luggage and one hanging garment bag. Use these to carry your tools to the set and arrive as a professional. Use one piece of luggage as a carry-on and have one available for check-in. Be mindful, however, not to pack valuable and critical items in your checked luggage as it has the possibility of getting lost. You will not need to take all of your tools with you to every shoot. The requirements will vary by client and market. You will learn from your agent and from experience which items you will need. The following pages include a list of the general requirements for your model tote bag:

MODEL TOTE AND TRAVEL REQUIREMENTS

Bra/Strapless Bra *(seamless and underwire flesh tone, black)*

Body Stocking and Tube Top *(flesh tone)*

Flattering One-Piece Swimsuit

Slips & Camisoles *(flesh tone, white and black)*

Dress/Underarm Shields

Hosiery *(sandal foot, flesh-toned, white, off-white, black opaque/sheer)*

Sports Socks *(white)*

Lightweight Robe *(for changing)*

Clean White T-Shirt

Shoes
*black and brown evening strappy, boot and loafer
white, bone, brown, black variety of heels and flats
clean white ked-type sneakers*

Accessories
*scarves
belts
jewelry (rhinestone, pearl, gold, silver)*

Hygiene Necessities
tampons
panty liners
deodorant
baby powder
nail kit
sewing kit
travel iron
lotion
lightly scented perfume

Make-up Bag
tweezers
assorted brushes
skin care items
eye drops/ contact solution/sunglasses
sponges
eyelash curler
concealer
foundation
loose powder (translucent)
pressed powder (for touch-ups)
blush (cool and warm)
2 eye pencils
4 assorted eye shadows (light, medium and dark)
2 lip liners (cool and warm)
2 lip sticks (cool and warm)
mascara (black and brown)
neutral nail polish
nail file
razor/hair remover
toothbrush, toothpaste, mouthwash, dental floss, mints

Hair Products
brush/comb
styling products (gel, spray, mousse, etc.)
black small hair ties
hair pins
travel hair dryer

Portfolio and Composite-Cards

Date Book, Contact Book, Casting/Booking Log, Agency Vouchers, Pen

Reading Material/Inspirational Music
(emotional preparation for shooting and performing)

Cell Phone/Pager

Water, Snack, Vitamins

Identification/Passport and Money *(when traveling at least $100.00)*

Camera

42.   PREPARE FOR LIFE BACKSTAGE.

After you have created your model tote you will be prepared for life backstage, where anything and everything can happen. You will be expected to make fast changes. Dressers will be backstage to help you change, however, ultimately you are responsible for getting into your outfit and getting out onto the runway on time. Having your model tote prepared will help you to have the correct undergarment, a safety pin if needed, tape to alter the bust line, or to tape a garment down for any of your changes. You must develop a fast system, and discuss this system with your dresser to execute your changes effectively. Generally, unbuttoning shirts and jackets ahead of time, just enough to slip on and off easily is a good idea. You must pay close attention to your line-up position and to how long you have in between changes, so that you know when you have a quick 30-60 second change or when you have more time to prepare.

"You've got to believe deep down inside that you're destined to do great things." *Joe Paterno*

43. PREPARE FOR LIFE ON THE ROAD.

Incorporate your travel sense in carrying with you only the essentials that keep you prepared for life. You must have a way of paying bills; communicating with people and protecting yourself while you are traveling. A cell phone and a laptop might be wise investments so that you can be connected with people who are important to you in an instant while you are traveling. It is easy to get caught up in the whirlwind life of traveling across the world as a model, however, if you cultivate behaviors to keep you grounded, the transition will run more smoothly.

"Do what you can, where you are, with what you've got." *Theodore Roosevelt*

44. CREATE YOUR PORTFOLIO AND MODEL CARD.

Collect any publicity and advertising pieces you receive from magazines, newspapers, brochures, as well as photographs, which can be used professionally. Show these photos to your agent and talk about which photographs best represent you, and which photographs will work best for your market. You and your agent will then choose which photographs will go in your portfolio and on your model composite card. If you do not have photographs, your agent will help you find a photographer to capture your style and get your card and book started. The following two pages include a sample composite:

Jennifer McLeod

**Photographs by Richard Petrillo &
Kristoff Brokowski
Front of Composite Card**

Back of Composite Card

45. STAY CURRENT AND EVOLVE.

Aim to update your look on an annual basis. Ideally you will update twice a year. You must constantly be shooting and working to evolve and re-create yourself. Discuss any major changes such as hair color, drastic haircuts, piercing, and surgeries with your agent prior to making these changes. Clients, and the markets, respond well to models that are ahead of the curve and aware of what's "hot" now. Keep your personal style and your pictures reflective of the fact that you are a model of today, not years ago.

"We must always change, renew, rejuvenate ourselves, otherwise we harden." *Goethe*

V.

Tips for Networking and Staying in Touch

Jennifer McLeod

46.   BE A SAVVY NETWORKER.

Get involved in your community. Volunteer for projects supported by fashion, arts, advertising and entertainment. Attend fundraisers, benefits and get-togethers sponsored by your agency. This is a great way to show your face and support to the people who are in your community. Remember to speak with people who have both the ability and resources to make a positive difference.

"You have to expect things of yourself before you can do them." *Michael Jordan*

47. ASSOCIATE WITH INDUSTRY PROFESSIONAL ORGANIZATIONS.

There may be several professional local organizations within your community dedicated to bringing together members of the fashion, arts, advertising and entertainment population. Research the Internet, phone books and talent agencies to learn of such associations in your area. The Screen Actors Guild and American Federation of Television and Radio Artists are good places to start.

"Hope is a waking dream." *Anonymous*

48. GO TO THE INTERNET TO FIND ADDITIONAL MODELING AGENCIES.

Check out the List of AFTRA/SAG Franchised Agencies. The Screen Actors Guild lists agencies that they franchise. Deal with agencies that are franchised by the Screen Actors Guild to ensure that you are dealing with a quality agent. The following websites include contact information regarding AFTRA and SAG: www.sag.org, www.aftra.com. You can also find agencies through www.modelnetwork.com and www.tearsheet.com.

"Why go unknown when you don't have to?" *Nicole*

49. DEVELOP A DATABASE OR FILE CATALOG OF ALL IMPORTANT INDUSTRY CONTACTS YOU MAKE.

Write down the date you met the person, where and what you talked about. This will serve you well later when the person calls you regarding work, or if you see the person again at an industry related event. You must be attentive to remembering names and faces. Use your Booking/Casting/Interview log to add to this file.

"You must be the change you wish to see the world." *Gandhi*

50. LEARN TO PROMOTE AND MARKET YOURSELF.

Study the promotion and marketing strategies of top models. Research successful marketing strategies through the Internet, magazines and books. Consider working in promotions, or some related field of marketing during down time so that you can learn first-hand how to promote and market yourself. Capitalize on publicity. Exposure in the appropriate light will help your career tremendously. Once you are ready, hire a publicist.

"Begin at once to live." *Seneca*

STAY IN TOUCH.

Please share your comments, suggestions and successes.

Send correspondence to:

50 Tips for Breaking into the Modeling Industry

c/o Jennifer McLeod

4802 E. Ray Road #23-130

Phoenix, AZ 85044

Thanks for your time and good luck!

REFERENCE & ADDITIONAL READING

Anderson, Peggy M. (1995). <u>Attitude is Everything</u>. Lombard, IL. Successories Publishing. (Quotations)

Boyd, Marie Anderson. (1997). <u>Model</u>. New York, NY: Peter Glenn Publications.

Hayes, Lucky, Stein, Elayne. (1990). <u>"That's No Way To Act!" A Handbook For Commercial And Film Actors</u>. Talent Builders International.

Kerr, Judy. (1997.) <u>Acting is Everything An Actor's Guidebook for a Successful Career in Los Angeles</u>. Studio City, CA: September Publishing.

Newton, Mack, St. George, Michele. (1997). <u>A Path to Power A Masters Guide to Conquering Crisis</u>. Phoenix, AZ: NTKD Publishing.

Ragnarsson, Huggy (1998). <u>Elite Street The Elite Model Look: A Fashion and Style Manual</u>. New York: Universe Publishing in Association with Elite Special Projects.

Rose, Yvonne and Tony. (1997). <u>Is Modeling For You?</u>. Los Angeles, CA: Phoenix, AZ: Amber Books.

Shanahan, John M. (1999). <u>The Most Brilliant Thoughts of All Time (In Two Lines or Less)</u>. New York, NY: Harper Collins Publishers, Inc. (Quotations)

www.fordmodels.com

www.modelnews.com. (2000). <u>Free Insiders Report On The Modeling Industry</u>. Geri Craig Publications.

Young, Kate (2001) <u>Vogue Hollywood Style Guide</u>.

Notes

Notes

Notes

Notes

Notes

Notes

Notes

Notes

Notes

Notes

Notes

Notes

Notes

Notes

Notes

Notes

Notes

ABOUT THE AUTHOR

Jennifer McLeod, Professional Model and Actress, has modeled in over 175 cities, including New York, New York; Los Angeles, California; Chicago, Illinois; Toronto, Canada; and Nassau, Bahamas. Her work includes companies such as Ford models, Ogilvy & Mather Advertising, Nordstrom, Dillard's, AT&T and Ebony Magazine. As a Certified Broadcaster she served as the morning show radio producer for a station among the Top Twenty in the national market. She holds a Bachelor of Science degree in Business Marketing and is a member of the Screen Actors Guild Book Pals Foundation-Performing Artists for Literacy in the Schools.